The Poetry of
James

by
James B. Sinclair PhD
Emeritus Professor

authorHOUSE®

AuthorHouse™
1663 Liberty Drive
Bloomington, IN 47403
www.authorhouse.com
Phone: 1 (800) 839-8640

Published by AuthorHouse   06/20/2017

ISBN: 978-1-5246-9624-5 (sc)
ISBN: 978-1-5246-9625-2 (hc)
ISBN: 978-1-5246-9623-8 (e)

Library of Congress Control Number: 2017909324

Print information available on the last page.

Dedication

In memory of my mother

Helen (Thompson Sinclair) Owens

$\mathscr{A}$cknowledgements

The first and most influencial person in my life and to whom just giving thanks is not enough was my mother, Helen M. (Thompson Sinclair) Owens. She received a Certificate In Journalism in 1925 after graduating from high school. She wanted to be a reporter. This was unusual for a woman at the time. However, she fell in love, married and started a family. She continued to practice her skills and published, with bylines, in a varietty of newspapers including the *Chicago Tribune*. She developed my interest in writing at an early age and I used these skills throughout my scientific and literary careers.

I modified some of my mother's poems and included them in this collection. I decided to try my hand at creative writing in 2012 after my retirement from a career in science. I registered for noncredit courses in 2013 given at the Oshner Lifelong Learning Center (OLLI) sponsored by the University of Illinois. One course was "The Writer's Café" given by Frank Chadwick and another was "Writing and Performing Poetry" given by John Palen. I registered for each course more than once. As a result I have published a memoir "My Name Is James" and seven poems. These poems are included in this collection. I thank OLLI and those men and women in the classes who helped develop my potential for these accomplishments.

My mother left a notebook of her unpublished poems. I modified and changed some of them and they are also included in this collection.

Special thanks go to Glen Hartman who helped me use a computer effectively and in preparing the photographs of the drawings.

$\mathscr{P}$reface

This book of poetry is a compilation of poems written during the same period (2012 -2017) as my memoir titled "My Name Is James." Some of the poems were published in various journals and some appeared for the first time in my memoir. The innate ability of writing poems was discovered after I retired from a career in science. I was over eighty years old when I began writing both the memoir and the poetry. This year I am now ninety.

I retired from the University of Illinois as an Emeritus Professor in 2002. My title was: Professor of International Plant Pathology. I was a member of a research team assigned to assist in the development of soybeans as a food crop in developing countries, partcularly India. My appointment began in 1968. I traveled to over forty countries, professionally, before I retired.

In preparation for retirement I took docent training at both the Krannert Art Museum and the Spurlock Cultural Museum on the University of Illinois campus. I gave tours at both museums until it became difficult for me as I aged, I now serve on the Board of Directors of both museums. It was then I looked for another challenge.

I decided to take some of the non-credit courses offered by the OLLI program at the university. This is where I learned to write in the active voice and discovered my ability to write poetry. I continue to enroll in these courses when offered.

I have included all of the poems written during the past four or five years. Some of them are good and others not so good. I leave the reader to decide.

Similarly, I leave it to the reader to decide whether or not the art work is any good. I was astounded to find I was able to make drawings to accompany some of the poems. I showed some of the drawings to friends and relatives who encouraged me to include them in this work.

The poems are arranged in fifteen categories.

$\mathscr{L}$ist of Original Images

Table of Contents

Ancient History

Gods And Goddesses

Where are the Olympian gods and godesses?
They were here a few centuries ago,
controlling the lives and fates of those who believed,
and interfering with the comings and goings of mankind.

The finest temples, elaborate shrines and elegant statues
built for the devoted to worship and adore.
Athena, the sophisticated goddess of wisdom and the arts,
was housed in the grandest way, presented in ivory and gold.

We remember Poseidon, the moody god of the sea,
and Apollo, god of the sun and music.
Then there was Dionysus, the joyful god of wine,
and Zeus, ruler of the world and king of the gods.

The royal Olympian family consisted of twelve,
who lived majestically, endowed with human frailties,
sometimes providing chosen humans with godly powers.
They remained continually young and death never came.

Where has this royal court and courtiers gone?
They never left the mount the Cyclops built.
They still influence us with their stories,
as did the prophets of religions now followed.

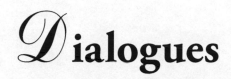

Dialogues

$\mathcal{T}$able For Two

"I am sorry I'm a little late, but traffic was horrible."

"It's okay, you're always late."

"That's not true. I'm not always late. Besides, not everyone is as punctual as you are."

"I went ahead and ordered our drinks and a plate of hors d'oeuvres you like."

"Thank you, but I was thinking about ordering something different tonight,
but it's okay."

"It's not too late to change it, it's up to you. "

"No, it's okay. Have you also decided what we'll have for dinner?"

"Oh, don't be so bitchy. I just want us to enjoy the evening. Order what you want. This is our anniversary."

"Well, I want to order something special, something I haven't had before.
Am I limited on price?"

"Oh stop! Get what you want. Would you like some soup? They have some specials. "."

"Yes, their French onion is always good. I'll have that."

"I think I'll have that, too."

"I am debating between raost duck, or maybe the halibut. Fish is healthier for you, but I'll have the duck. It's always good."

"That was fast, you usually take forever to make up your mind."

"I do not."

"I'll also have the duck. "

The Last Supper

"Hello honey, I'm home."

"How'd your day go?"

"The usual. Thank God it's Friday. What's for supper? Whatever it is, it sure smells good."

"I went to lunch with Mona, we did a little shopping and then I spent the rest of the afternoon at her place."

"You and Mona sure have become close these past few months."

"Yeh, we have so much in common. She's like the sister I never had. I really like her.
Come and sit down. I have something to tell you."

"Wow! Roast beef and all the trimmings. Thank you. It looks great. To be a bit trite,
it looks good enough to eat."

"Enjoy it, it may be our last supper together."

"What? What do you mean?"

"I'm going to say it straight out - I want a divorce."

"You did say "divorce" didn't you?"

"Yes."

"Oh! My God, why? Aren't you happy? God knows I've tried to be a good husband."
"It's not your fault, it's - well - it's hard to say. Mona and I are in love and she wants me to move in with her."

"I don't believe it. I don't know what to say."

"You don't have to say anything. We are planning on my moving at the end of the month.
I've already talked to our lawyer."

"There's nothing I can do to change your mind?"

Death

$\mathcal{D}$on't Weep For Me

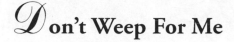

(Based on a poem of Helen M.Owens)

Don't weep for me if I'm not here
to share this time with you,
for I have shared many happy times
much more than was my due.

I've seen the golden sunrise
with dear ones kind and true
and saw the great red oak
turn to a golden hue.

A silver path upon the lake
shimmering like glistening stones
made a shiny way
for me to walk upon.

I've reached the heights of ecstasy
known the feelings of despair.
I've had one who gave me love
friends who deeply cared.

All in all my life was full,
great wonders did I see.
Weep not for me as I depart,
just remember me, remember me.

$\mathcal{I}$ Never Knew My Father

I never knew my father
who died when I was five.

There was no substitute
to discipline and to guide.

Grandad was a model
to follow and to emulate.

Though he cared for and protected me,
there was no love to share.

I longed for a loving father
to confide and to teach me,

A dad to instruct me about life
and what it means to be a man.

I Saw Death Last Night

I woke and heard an old man coughing in the House of Illness.

The sump water rushed to be aired again on wet cement.

The wind dipped its fingers in the lake causing ripples
and then it played with newly born leaves of a nearby tree.

I saw death last night, twice,
and walked in white lace with my brother
through a dirty street.

I saw a corpse lying face down in a snow bank,
another on the top of a garage, two men ran away,
I took off my white lace to call the police.

There was the impression of a cloven hoof in the sand.

The iris will have borne a purple babe by morning
and the white bells of the lily-of-the-valley will sway
with the playful breeze.

"God is in His heaven and all is well with the world."

The light flickers, but does not go out;
the handsome youth turns alone and restless,
but again sleeps as the early morning sun
pokes at the nesting birds in the big oak tree.

Palimpsest

Mother died.
She left a trunk of treasurers.

Greeting cards and letters
with stamps now collector's items.

One letter written by a rebel soldier
to his mother in Richmond.

A gold-tipped baton
used by my great-grandfather
to conduct his orchestra and choir.

My great-grandmother's cookbook
where she saved family records
by pasting clippings over the recipes.

Old photographs of great-grandparents and others
in a velvet covered album of family and friends,
and a child laid out in a coffin.

This is who I am today.

Previously published in: Pegasus, 2016. Summer/Autumn Issue. Kentucky
State Poetry Society: 28.

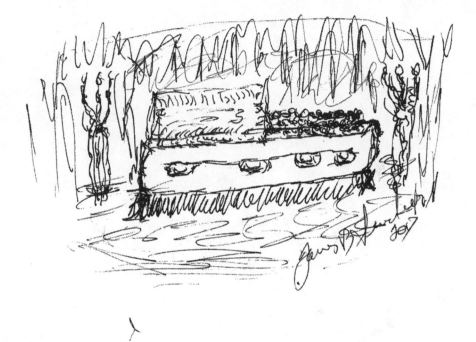

Where Did Great Grandma Go?

Where Did Great Grandma Go?

I was three.
Great-grandma died.
I didn't know her name.

She sat in her rocker
a doily on her head
when we visited.

Now she's lying down
in a big box
a doily on her head.

It can't be my great-grandma,
she would reach out
and hold me on her lap.

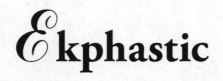

Ekphastic

Of Four Youth On A Bridge

An Ekphastic Poem In Response To Pelli Ohlstead's Photograph

*O*f Four Youth On A Bridge

The quiet of a flowing stream reflects from above
the attention of four innocent youth
not yet exposed to what the future will bring
but thinking, not sharing hopes and concerns.

One of them already knows,
without a father to guide him,
he alone will find the knowledge
needed to live well and love often.

Another questions her acceptability
to the girls in her class at school:
"Am I pretty? " "Is my hair the right color?"
"Do I wear the right shoes and clothes?"

The athletic type is already aware
of opportunities awaiting in the sports arena
which will bring honors and awards,
and scholarships through the years.

Alas, the orphan, alone except for his friends,
sees only a bleak future.
He hopes some day there will be
a special someone to love him.

They provide a potent mixture
of today's neophytes wondering about life,
not ready to travel in Charon's boat
to the other side.

Living will take them just so far,
not to the other side, but stopped midstream
to let them off to rest in green pastures and
and eventual sleep, then to be no more.

Family

y Father

(Based on a poem by Helen M. Owens)

Though you are gone like the breathe of a song,
your image will always remain.

Though you sleep and the earth enfolds you,
your image will always remain.

A friend upon whom one can depend,
a treasure not easily found.

I think of you with care on your brow
from toils, infirmaries and worry.

You're now free of earth's many trials.
Your image will always remain.

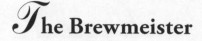The Brewmeister

In 1927 Prohibition was the law,
Mother and Dad were newlyweds
Investing in a bungalow
on Chicago's south side.

She was 18 and he 21,
first among their peers
to marry and have a home.

They had company every Saturday night.
Dad noted for his home brew
made in a converted bathtub
housed in a basement room.

He was a master of his craft,
bottling and capping the product
in clean containers, there to age.

Mother oft told the story
of how on a winter's night
they were awakened
by popping caps and flowing beer.

It was a mess for both to clean.
Mom blamed Dad for bottling
the homemade brew too soon.

There was not much left
for those friends and relative
to have a party that Saturday night.
A few from an earlier batch had to do.

Published previously in My Name Is James. 2017. AuthorHouse, IN

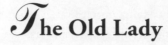The Old Lady

The old lady sits in her ancient chair
serving her through these many years
as a source of comfort and escape,
her friend, holding her near.

She reflects on things long gone
youth, marriage, and motherhood.
How quickly all these pass.

She watches the cycle among the young
who see them as new and exciting,
as if never happening to those now old.

She cherishes her childhood innocence
her marriage vows now reviewed
the ecstasy of the honeymoon and
learning to live with a caring man.

She muses about the concerns of youth,
the trials of parenthood and being ill
the death of loved ones still remembered
who provided strength and love through the years.

She has lived a life of joys and sorrows,
hope and regrets, problems solved,
unrealized dreams, great parties,
sumptuous dinners and family reunions.

She sees the young still experiencing,
not concerned in things now past.
Their surprised about tales she tells
of survival and her memorable years.

She rejoiced when her children succeeded
in their endeavors and lofty aims.
Their visits back to tell of these joys,
which she helped them to obtain.

You, Old House

You, Old House

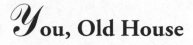

You, old house, now nearing ninety
built by the hands of a family now gone,
who housed four generations of kin,
now have new owners to share
your comfort and protection from the rest.

Your many windows let in the light,
to view the great lake nearby,
to observe the wild life residing there,
to watch the water from the flowing well
meandering to the sandy shore.

The great shade trees and evergreens
gathered about your hearty frame
providing shelter from the summer sun
and high winds that oft abound,
then to display the kaleidoscope of autumn.

You've witnessed birth and death,
sickness and healing of oh so many,
and delights, celebrations, and parties,
picnics and feasts, of happy days;
an unwritten history of joys and sorrows.

You stood stalwartly against storms and floods
protecting those within from adversity,
a haven for those who had so little,
a retreat for those who prospered,
not caring who they were.

You now care for others as in the past,
never tiring, a little worn and weathered,
still providing forever renewing generations,
waiting on those yet to arrive,
a long life well lived, a legacy to recall.

From: My Name Is James. 2017. AuthorHouse, Bloomington, IN.

Ghazal

What If I Told You Stories Of Mine

(modified ghazal)

What if I told you stories of mine?
Would you believe me? Would you believe me?

Of visiting the gods on Olympus mount.
Would you believe me? Would you believe me?

Of trekking up and into the foothills of the Himalayas.
Would you believe me? Would you believe me?

Of feeling the heat of Hell where the devil dwells.
Would you believe me? Would you believe me?

Of seeing lepers begging in a market place.
Would you believe me? Would you believe me?

Of angels singing to me in a heavenly realm.
Would you believe me? Would you believe me?

Of drinking bourbon with 10,000-year-old ice.
Would you believe me? Would you believe me?

Of sirens chanting to bring about my demise.
Would you believe me? Would you believe me?

Do I dream to much? Are these really fantastic?
Would you believe me? Would you believe me?

Haiku

Haiku

. A handsome youth smiles
muscular, slim and graceful
such inviting eyes

. Alone in my garden
my constant companions are
the flashing fireflies

Black clouds roar and send
ragged flashes streaks of white
announcing a storm

Fish stir the water
in a clear lake of deep blue
reflecting white clouds

Lilacs and roses
of different hues and scents
please all my senses.

Our constant blue dome
cannot provide protection
from the shooting stars.

The old dying stag
promises sustenance to
waiting scavengers

The sacred icon
promises us forgiveness
with true repentance

Winds howl in a rage
above the now barren forest
the're no leaves to blow

Humor

A Quiet Evening

It's been a peaceful night.
little of interest on the tube.
They're predicting snow,
more than two inches.

I ignore the commercials
and station breaks.
The advertisements
are mind-numbing.

My chair is cozy and warm.
The arm and leg rests
are relaxing me.
I'm ready to go to sleep.

I'm on a diet, no snacks,
no sugar-laced drinks.
Too soon for bed,
I'll wake too early.

I succumb to yawns,
the bedroom calls.
I barely have time to change
into my night clothes.

Once in bed my mind awakens.
A whirl of thoughts begin about my day,
over and over of to dos for tomorrow.
I cannot sleep.

Crows Are The Mosr Maligned Creatures

Crows Are The Most Maligned Creatures

Crows are the most maligned of all the birds.
Their feathers are black, they have beady, bright eyes.
They tend to gather in large flocks without reason
in towns and cities soiling their surroundings.

Crows thrive on carrion in the field and on hghways
and domesticated grain during harvest.
Therefore, acing as both servant and pest,
playing a roll in the balance of nature.

They are noisy, and pesky, and crude.
Their unmelodious song is squawking and, in unison,
penetrating and harsh. Loud noises disperse them
but they soon return to continue their concert.

The crow often appears as a familiar to a witch or warlock
carrying out the intentions of their dark and evil soul.
Crows are associated with ghosts and goblins during
Halloween celebrations and black magic rituals.

Crows play an important and interesting roll in the fine arts,
Van Gogh painted crows in many of his scenes of maturng grain.
Throughout history a drawing of a crow implies the presence of
evil in a drama, painting or poem.

Unfortunately, crow never found a place in international cuisine.

$\mathcal{M}$y Friend Foley[*]

Oh, what would I do
without my friend Foley.
He is with me night and day,
always a close companion.

He grasps me in an intimate manner,
gently holding me close
with only the slightest of pressure.
Sometimes I'm not aware of his presence.

He is a dedicated servant
always there when I need him,
providing instant service.
I couldn't go on without him.

He pushes against me
if I forget to return the friendship.
He sometimes drinks too much,
it is then I must care for him.

[*] A Foley is a urinary catheter

The Basketball Game

The family decides to watch the game
on a week night with no school tomorrow.
The television hangs over the fireplace
and there is a large overstuffed sofa to share.
Mother decides the children can watch the first half
and she'll make popcorn.

The fire is lit.

A small flame, a wiff of smoke, the fire is about out.
Between the two children, now fast asleep,
a bowl lays tilted, empty, but for a few kernels.
The sleeping parents are unaware of the blank screen
and technical noise of a signed-off station.

Something awakens them.

The first half of the unwatched game is long over,
the home team losing by a large margin.
The children are sent off to bed without a word.
The parents turn off the television and bank the fire.

Dad turns to Mom and asks: "Who won?

$\mathscr{B}$utch

(Based on a poem by Helen M. Owens)

My Butch is not a thoroughbred,
he doesn't have a pedigree,
he may not have a shapely head,

but he still suits me.

His ears are not as long as some dogs,
his tail is not cut as others my be,
his brown coat is marbled with white,

but he still suits me.

His feet are big and clumsy
as he goes on walks with me,
and doesn't repond to each command,

but he still suits me.

His brown eyes are soft and gentle
and show his love for me.
He is funny mutt,

but he still suits me.

Farewell, Dear Friend

Farewell, dear friend,
I loved you once in bygone days.
Even now my thoughts remind me
of the love I had for you...

This memory of our unspoken love
still haunts me to this day,
as I try to write in poetic form,
of thoughts as yet revealed to few.

Your heart knew mine,
our thoughts were one,
we anticipated each other's actions,
and laughed when such events occurred.

What force destroyed this love?
Was it just a habit, born to be broken?
Were we so encased in our defensive shields,
too blind, too afraid to consummate this love?

We parted with the truth untold.
We never spoke again.
Does he ever think of me
and those few most cherished days?

From: My Name Is James. 2017. AuthorHouse, Bloomington, IN.

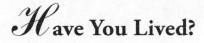 ave You Lived?

(Based on a poem by Helen M. Owens)

Have you known the handclasp of a friend?
One who was always there,
upon who you could always rely
to help, to trust and to care?

Have you known the ecatasy of a kiss
that stayed with you through the years?
Have you known sorrow that tore your heart?
Have you known deadly fears?

Have you ever heard the laughter
that comes from a child's joy?
Have you seen a baby chuckle and grin
at seeing a bright new toy?

Have you made a courageous sacrifice
done just to please another?
If you missed anyone of these
you really haven't lived at all.

$\mathcal{L}$ove Unspoken

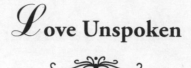

There is a love unspoken
of one man for another
labeled "comrade" in battle
and "best buddy" in peace.

Love and lust are confused
sometimes mixed to confound
especially in our early years
when hormones tend to guide us.

This shared affection
expressed in most subtle ways,
oft in secret moments
when others are not present.

From: My Name Is James. 2017. AuthorHouse, Bloomington, IN.

My First Boyfriend

I was born gay!

"How do you know?

From a story my mother told me.

When I was not yet five,

my playmate from next door

was about to enter kindergarten.

without me!

I was heartbroken and

grieved not realizing

I was in love!

Mother convinced the principal

to let me attend school

with my first boyfriend!

From: My Name Is James. 2017. AuthorHouse, Bloomington, IN

*M*y Wish For You

I wish you health, but take care of it.

I wish you good luck, but we make it.

I wish you wealth, but not what it will buy.

I wish you a great love, but it needs to be shared.

I wish you compassion for those around you.

The Desire

(Based on a poem by Helen M. Owens)

If we might for one brief hour
forget we are so far apart
and lie within each other's arms
with mouth to mouth and heart to heart.

For just one hour from our lives
to sink unchained from passion deep
and be cast upon the farthest shore
to live embraced in tender sleep.

The Fragile Rose

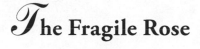The Fragile Rose

I gently broke a fragile rose
from a thornless bough;
I held it close, I smelled the scent,
it was my love for thou.

Although it bled, it showed no pain.
It gladly gave of itself,
but soon another love did pass
and took that gift from me.

He carried it just a little way,
then dropped it to the ground.
He did not know that what he had
could not be found again.

The bush still has a wound to show.
Now guarded by a thorn,
a fuller bud, just now born,
no more to be marred.

I want to pick this rose anew,
again to hold it close,
but will it let me capture it,
only again to be taken away?

From: My Name Is James. 2017. AuthorHouse, Bloomington, IN.

Memories

Being An Outsider

$\mathcal{B}$eing An Outsider

My parents were young and naive,
both innocent virgins when they married,
limited by family, church and school
even in the time of the "roaring 20's."

The first born child was to be a boy
according to my father's fondest wishes.
My mother so wanted it to be a girl.
No predictive procedures were there to tell.

The difficult birth, which came too soon,
began a month before I was due.
Born in the winter near Christmas Day,
an unexpected holiday gift in blue.

At birth I was a weak and sickly child
not a healthy, strong, and robust "all boy"
as envisioned in the imagination of my father
and his dreams of a sports-minded, viable son.

Father's genes gave me a tall and manly body;
my mother's a kind and sensitive soul.
Uncoordinated from the start
sporting games were not meant for me.

The love of music, the arts and ballet,
plants and flowers, movies and men
would guide me through the struggles
of a profession and adverse judgements.

I was an outsider trying to escape the limits
imposed by colleagues and acquaintances,
but not by supportive family members,
close friends and lovers.

Carnival In New Orleans

Carnival in New Orleans

Beginning on the Twelfth Night
celebrating the arrival of three Zoroastrians
dressed in elaborate gowns and headgear
riding camels across a desert wasteland
to bestow rich gifts on a newly-born baby boy.

From this festive night of parties and cakes
to the day before Ash Wednesday (Fat Tuesday)
there are festive gatherings and parades
of sparkling chariots carrying gifts for all.

The crowds beg for presents from god-like creatures
riding majestically on gaudy floats
carrying chests of gold-colored trinkets and beads,
candy and favors, cheap coins called doubloons

Like ancient priests and parishioners
we raise our hands from the streets below
not asking for godly guidance or special favors,
but begging for a trinket, a coin, a bit of something sweet,
received from these generous givers.

Ask and it shall be given,
give me that which I desire,
to hold, treasure, collect, and to recall this time
with no thought of repayment or thanks.

From: My Name Is James. 2017. AuthorHouse, Bloomington, IN.

rowing Up

Once I had a family large
who guided me through my youth.
Soon I was shown a path to follow
and so with youthful thoughts and stamina
did that love direct me to my destiny.

$\mathcal{M}$y Books

Of all the Christmases now remembered,
through my life of eighty years,
there is one in which a gift was given,
of three bound books in a fancy box.
A present to read and treasure,
to cherish and to love throughout my life.

These volumes were the embryo of
a collection developed through the years
of other gifts and purchases
ever growing in subject and diversity.

The largest gift was given in my teens,
by grandad, a reader and collector
of many books of great variety:
history, philosophy, witchcraft and the black arts,
Shakespeare, Spinosa, and Dostoevsky, and
renditions of famous prints and paintings.

The library was with me wherever I did go,
sometimes packed in boxes or tied with string,
like true friends, waiting for me to settle down,
to be a source of thoughts and achievements.

At last displayed in a permanent place
on many shelves waiting to be read again,
to browse, to seek information, or find a quote,
to stimulate and bring enjoyment once again.

I love these aging books so faithful,
a storehouse for constant renewal.
Now in my waning years,
it is time to pass them on to others,
who will love them as I have
and use them as they're meant to be.

Ravages Of Time

Like the striations in a canyon wall,
layer upon layer mapping the past,
then slowly to be washed away
there to reveal the child we were.

Synapses which have formed
for conformity and remembering,
these too begin to erode
as the river of aging flows.

Finally as all is rinsed away
no record is left behind
to tell the story of a life well lived
unless it's saved in writing or in rhyme.

The Lamp On The Marble Top Table

The Lamp On The Marble Top Table

The lamp on the marble top table
was located in a conspicuous place
in the Victorian-furnished living room
of my great grandmother's fine home.

I was only a youngster, just beginning to walk,
seeing this lamp for the first time.
Now I was lifted to see her lying in her casket
veiled with a sheer fabric of white.

As was the custom of the time
the casket was placed in this great room
where draperies were drawn with
only the light from the lamp lit the gloom.

The next time I saw this lamp of pewter and glass
was in my grandmother's living room
now on a hand-carved, four-legged table
without a marble top.

It stood before a large window
providing light from the Victorian lamp,
a conversation piece, much admired
by relatives, guests and especially me.

There it remained for over half a century
witnessing the joys and sorrows of generations,
showing signs of accidents and wear,
of constant cleaning and repair.

Then grandad's stroke made them move,
the household goods were sold,
the lamp stayed within the family,
carefully carried to its new home.

It no longer looked so elegant and fine
missing the crystal orb on the top,
a glass panel replaced with one that did not match,
and now painted an off-white.

When grandmother died the lamp was passed
to my mother to care for and cherish.
It was placed on a small, faux marble table top
in front of her living room window.

There is remained until it was given to me
now a desk lamp providing light
for activities of a professor and consultant.
It served me well as it had the others before me.

That grand old lamp is not worth much,
now owned by grandmother's namesake,
who will love and care for it
as did those who have preceded us.

The Longing

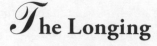

I long for the days of my youth
when the family designed and built
the house on the lake
and the many summers there.

Now only in my thoughts and dreams
I recall the willing efforts to raise it
on pritine land adjacent to the
unspoiled lake of clear water.

This was once Blackhawk land.
They left arrow heads and axes,
graves and burial mounds
to remind us of their presence.

The house was abandoned
after four generations,
sold and moved up on a hill
to serve and shelter other families.

The water in the lake became corrupt
with effluent from farms and septic tanks.
Where fish and turtles once abound
only weeds and alga bloom now flourish.

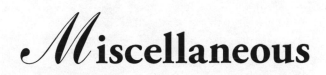

Miscellaneous

$\mathcal{B}$est Meal Of The Day

I look forward each morning
to breakfast, the best meal of the day,
carefully planned and tested long ago
to bring balance to my diet,
keeping calories low.

No more bacon, eggs, pancakes with syrup,
no sweet breads or buttered toast,
but now with oatmeal, fresh fruit,
skimmed milk, sugar-free jam and
whole wheat bread.

No coffee, tea, coke or whole milk,
but a glass of water before each meal.
Lunch and dinner are not so varied,
turkey sandwich, fruit and water at noon,
a high protein dinner and low-calorie dressing.

Sometimes a raisin-oatmeal cookie for dessert.

Daily Battles Well Fought

Daily Battles Well Fough

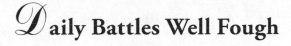

As the sun pushes away the thick, dark clouds
resisting being broken and diminished
having dominated the night skies
bringing an unwanted cold spring rain,

A bleary-eyed boy, still awakening
from his encounter with a fiery dragon,
plods along the pasture's edge
avoiding the land-mined puddles.

He is headed for the nebulous mass of
dirty white and brown bivouacked cows
sharing their warmth in the morning chill
giving off white vapors from breathe and bodies.

The boy must disjoint this smoky cluster,
force them to move along a familiar trail
to where they'll be stripped of their product
to serve the demands of their captors.

$\mathscr{D}$riving Instructions

Stop! Yield! Caution!
School Crossing, School Zone.

No Parking, Parallel Parking,
Private Parking, Metered Parking,
Twenty Minute Parking,
Handicap Parking, $200 Fine.

Car Wash, Car Repair,
Tire Rotation, Tire Repair.
Lubrication, Lube Job, Oil Change,
Radiator Flush, Battery Change.

Unleaded, Unleaded Plus, Premium Unleaded,
Diesel.

Antifreeze, Windshield Wash.

Joining A Fraternity

College greeted me with open arms,
"You are welcomed, come and learn."
Three Greek letters then followed.

The fraternity boys shook my hand
"You are welcomed, come and live."
in the traditions of the past.

Now branded, forever wearing the pin,
from now on identified by it.
I've become one of them, no longer me

On Creative Writing

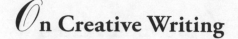

I learned about the rhythm of writing,
never to use the passive voice.
Rhyming is not necessary,
but a useful tool in thought expression.

Give some details about the characters
make them alive.
Only write about selected details that
add to the story line, but not too many.

Write every day with realistic goals.
Join a writing group or two to obtain
positive feedback and literary support.
Be kind to yourself, but steady and ruthless.

Always respect your own purposes.
Rewrite and review, set aside and return.
As Polonius once said "this above all"
apply your ass to the chair.

$\mathscr{T}$he Docent

All the lights are on and the galleries lite.
The great doors unlocked and opened.
It is quiet in the art museum
where great and not so great works
have rested through the night.

The docent awaits for the arrival
of an appointed group
to view these collected works and
to listen to the docent's explanations.
The noise of leather soles and
pointed heels breaks the silence.

The small group of viewers arrive
with chatter, giggles and a laugh or two.
The docent greets them and then
there is silence. It is quiet again
except for a few muted exchanges.

The rules of conduct are given and
a short history of the collection.
"Follow me please to the first gallery."
The group begins to flow to gallery one
where the quiet of the museum
is again interrupted by soles and heala

The well-versed docent provides
an interpretation of selected paintings and stone
in one gallery after another.
The docent stands, as per protocol,
on one side of each exhibited work
so visitors may fully view the artists's effort.

The docent asks at each stop
"Are there any questons?"
Occasionally one amongst the group,
with some knowledge of the item viewed,
will ask an intelligent question and may
make an appropriate comment or two.

At the end of the conduced tour
of bronze, canvas and glass
through the centuries and schools,
the docent thanks the group for their attention,
a round of applause and appreciation is given.

Another group is waiting
for the docent's tour and talk.
There will be more tours to give this day,
there is a group of high schoolers
free from the confines of their formal classes.

It is only by the presence of people
that the museum becomes alive and lives.
The docent is likewise stimulated by the visitors
who give a different interpretation or a
new insigfht into the work being viewed.

The day is over ad the doors are closed.
The docent signs out and leaves
as the lights go out, gallery by gallery.
On the way home the docent thinks,
I hope the visitors learned something today.

What If I Told You Stories Of Mine

(modified ghazal)

What if I told you stories of mine?
Would you believe me? Would you believe me?

Of visiting the gods on Olympus mount.
Would you believe me? Would You believe me?

Of trekking up and into the foothills of the Himalayas.
Would you believe me? Would you believe me?

Of feeling the heat of Hell where the devil dwells.
Would you believe me? Would you believe me?

Of seeing lepers begging in a market place.
Would you believe me? Would you believe me?

Of angels singing to me in a heavenly realm.
Would you believe me? Would you believe me?

Of drinking bourbon with 10,000-year-old ice.
Would you believe me? Would you believe me?

Of sirens chanting to bring about my demise.
Would you believe me? Would you believe me?

Do I dream too much? Are these really fanticies?
Would you believe me? Would you believe me?

Music

The Last Movement Of Handel's Water Music

Life again begins to flow
being dormant in a quiet,
desperate and decaying heart,
arising with the Water Music.

Out comes the love of mankind,
the love of each new individual's
inner beauty and each person's wonder,
and above all, their life and living.

Forgiveness leaps forth and
embraces my enemies and all
those who are jealous and
envious of my accomplishments.

My heart loves and forgives
those who slander and chop at it.
The outside may be ugly and scared,
but the inside is still soft and kind.

Nature

A Battle That Never Ends

The sun did not shine that day,
it was dark inside and out,
in the middle of summer.
I knew it was still there.

Clouds covered and hid the sky
hovering over my world
as a heavy black velvet cloak
determined to stay.

The dark monsters began to move
awakening from a deep sleep.
A strong west wind was called to battle
to move them on their way.

There were flashes as from cannon fire,
explosions from hand grenades and land mines,
all the noises of a fierce battle.
The wounded clouds roiled and resisted.

The clouds sent long fingers to the earth
grasping at anything to hold,
twisting and turning in all directions
finding nothing on which to anchor.

The battle ended with the monsters in retreat.
The wind pushed them on their way.
The clouds in revenge released its water
to flood the land below.

At the end of the mightty encounter
a quiet but damaged land was left behind.
The sun appeared giving light and warmth.
It was still there.

A Broken Limb

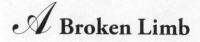A Broken Limb

A broken branch hangs loose
still attached to its trunk
still connected, still alive.

Can it be repaired, made whole again?
Shall we brace it, hold it in place?
Reaching out as it did before.

Or should it be removed
leaving a scar reminding us
of the tragedy of a broken limb?

From: American Poet. 2016. Eber and Wein, New Freedom, PA. 251.

April 2014

This April was a distinctive month
filled with special days:
April Fool's and Pascua Florida days
began the parades of notables.

The day of the full moon came next
which turned from black and white to pink
in the early morning hours when
most of us were regrettably asleep.

Religious festivals determined by
phases of the moon and ancient calendars
were there to help remind many of their faith:
Palm Sunday, Good Friday, Passover and Easter.

More modern and notable days were honored:
Earth Day and National Arbor Day
to celebrate and preserve our natural heritage
so often abused for improvement and profit.

Before Spring Arrives

Charcoal colored crows and trees like dirty sponges.

Forested patches, twisted and bruised, sticking up
as frayed bristles on a dirty hair brush.

Listless streams giving birth to black sticks and debris
among syrupy, rolling bubbles flowing together as dark lava.

Oaks draped with gray mourning leaves from last summer.

A wet day, a road slipping over bulbous hollows, high and low,
spreading onto a rotten-planked bridge.

Decaying fence rails diminished by molded sawdust mounds.

A tired building looking for a place to lean,
stained and streaked with winter's scum.

The carcases of golden rod and cotton tell of a white and gold past.

Bony brown cows plodding through the soggy pastures.
Stagnant water in barnyard pools with long-legged pigs
resting quietly in their muddy bath.

Grey chimney smoke, like a mist, disappeared against
tattle-tale grey clouds bringing on the day.

From: The Best Poets of 2016. 2017. Eber and Wien, New Freedom, PA.

Dawn

The earth moves as a well-regulated machine
to reveal the first glow of a new day.
The bright, hot orb creeps into the bowl of night
to nourish with heat and light the waking planet.

It's those photons that sustain the vital forces
once begun in salty water near heated vents
where inanimate elements united and became organic,
creating life dependent on their energy for sustenance.

Perhaps is it the sun we should be worshiping
and thanking for its gift of life
as did so many past tribes and cultures,
but it is inanimate, without feeling.

Still we worship inanimate gods not seen,
or earthly god and goddesses of our own creation,
or humans proclaiming to be prophets of unseen gods.
Yet it's in the nature of humans that we do.

idnight Fantasy

(Modified after a poem by Helen M. Owens)

The moon reflected brilliantly the sun
to cast upon the midnight lake below
a clear, cool festival of light
through the atmosphere made bright.

Along the shoreline
where trees tall and gracious grow
all dressed in rustling coats of white
through the atmosphere made bright.

The tall and gracious trees glow and
look down into the silver mirror to gaze,
to wonder if their leafy tresses were placed and
to catch their shimmering reflections in the lake.

The trees looked down into the silvery mirror to gaze
before a rift of air from the shore stirred the water
taking the shimmering reflections away and
to wonder if their leafy tresses were placed.

Before a rift of air stirred the water from the shore
it rustled thorough the foliage on high
then moved as gently as a heave or sigh
driving the shimmering reflections away.

Snow

A sky filled with crystalline flakes
fluttering nonchalantly to their rest,
a gift from the dark grey clouds above,
releasing their captured dew to earth.

The wind then plays games with them,
scattering their delicate, weightless forms,
swirling in directions unintended,
soon finding a place to rest.

Such fine creations should do no harm,
yet in extraordinary numbers
cause havoc to pets and families,
blocking trails and roads, treads and tracks.

Each a weightless form of beauty
together can crush a neighbor's house,
break a sturdy limb, topple a great tree,
impede our travel and the unsightly hide.

The End Of Their World

Before me stands a great mother oak,
her many arms and fingers
held out to the sky
to present her buds, flowers and foliage.

She was once an embryo,
then a delicate pale shoot
rising from a womb-like seed
given by her nurturing mother.

She survived the trials of living:
drought, floods, storms and damaged limbs;
the ice and snow of winter and heat of summer;
attacks by insects and pathogens.

Once a year she takes a rest
having stored nutrients for her hibernation.
She creates new buds protecting leaves and flowers
and sheds her aging foliage.

The green pigment fads and soon disappears
revealing bright colors always there.
It's time for them to go
having survived their season of living.

The Equinoxes

The equinoxes cast their spells
on all of us, great and small.
Our ancestors knew them well,
worshiping these events with ritual.

The arrival of each comes as earth does tilt
bringing hope and joy four times a year.
Be it autumn or spring, winter or summer,
each announce the promise of new sensations.

We credit our life-giving sun for them,
but it is not the cause of fluctuating seasons,
but the wobble of our great blue marble
as it perpetually rolls about.

The Old Stag

The Old Stag

Some crows koww as dusk begins.
The vultures circle above.
A wilily wolf eyes its prey.
An old stag stumbles nearby.

The atmosphere is filled
with tense anticipation.
A rabbit and her young
scurry away through the grass.

The wolf has plans,
as it creeps through the brush,
to attack the vulnerable stag.
It watches the weakened prey stagger.

The woods become quiet.
All creatures alert and watching.
The kill is made with little effort.
Predators and scavengers arrive.

The Tornado

The Tornado

The sky is hidden with a blanket of black.
The clouds within toss, turn, and tumble
fighting for space in a crowded mass.
The clash begins with an electric flash
that splits the hoard with a roar.

Frozen tears fall to mark the start
of a more furious battle yet to come.
More roars and rumbles intensify.
Soon they begin the dance of the dervish,
swirling and turning, faster and faster.

Now is the time to begin the frenzied
dance of destruction on the land below,
where sirens herald its arrival
and trees bow to the rapid winds.
The wind screams like a lost freight train.

All run for shelter to protect and hide
when the hated fury of the great invader begins.
It beats and bangs, crushes and condenses,
throws and discards, crashes and destroys.
leaving death and destruction in its wake.

All is quiet and serene now.
Night abruptly turns to day.
Soon there is movement and cries for help.
People and animals arise stunned and afraid,
stumbling from the rubble left behind.

The Trees In My Garden

As I prepare to celebrate another Arbor Day
by planting a young tree each year.
I am perplexed as to what variety to select
in this replanted landscape so dear.

Mighty oaks first were placed at measured distance,
a parade of great trees with lofty crowns.
All my plans went well until the Ceratocystis fungus
found a new home and proceeded to take its toll.

Next came the graceful elm, which provided ample shade,
to replace each oak as it succumbed to the insidious disease.
In due course came a cousin of the oak wilt fungus and
brought death to all the elms, the Dutch elm disease.

Planting White Pine would surely stop these invaders,
but they too began to die because of the pine wilt nematode.
I still had to find another tree to replemish the landscape
and turned to the mighty deciduous ash.

Then the ash trees began to die, not from fungus or nematode,
but an insect larva called the Emerald Ash borer.
Down came the infested trees, one by one,
as well as the healthy ones yet to succumb.

I chose the fast-growing locust and swamp birc,.
not as elegant and tall as the others,
but with hardy resistance to fungus, nematode and borer.
Next year my landscape will be graced with them.

From: Illinois Forestry Association Newsletter, Chatham, IL., 2017 12:15

There Is Nothing There

There is no sky!
I cannot feel or gather it.
Nothing is obstructed by it.

If there is no sky,
Then what is it I see?
Is it a phantom or just a pigment?

The color disappears at night.
The sun changes the black of night
to blue again.

When storm clouds gather,
the blue disappears
to return when they clear.

Every living thing can see it.
It must be real.
Yet, there is nothing there.

When I Am Asked

When I am asked
about my graduate studies
I talk about my love of plants.

This was discovered as a lad of twelve
without many interests or friends.

My teacher planted some grapefruit seeds
in a pot of soil upon the sill.

I beheld the emergence of a living thing,
held within its sealed capsule,
rising from its burial in earth,
stretching out its baby leaves
to the sun and air it needed to grow.

I asked for some of those magic pebbles
to plant at home, then to watch and wait.
The resurrection came from a quiet sleep,
eager to produce another generation.

It made me wonder, even as in the smallest of seeds,
where was the blueprint of the ensuing trees
stored to direct and promote the growth
of this new generation.

From: My Names Is James. 2017. AuthorHouse, Bloomington, IN.

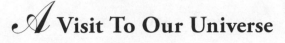 A Visit To Our Universe

Dark matter and black holes
hold our expanding universe together
by labeled forces described
but yet unknown.

Where time and space are the same,
neither of which can be seen or felt,
but we know they exist because
we take up space and travel through time.

We are told of expectations for life
in unfamiliar forms that might exist
on Mars or Saturn's moons
brought by meteors from supernovas long ago.

All this commotion can't be seen
when we view the Milky Way as a thing of beauty.
It is full of noise and fire, ever changing, creating
and destroying.
How naive to call it "heavenly."

It is more hellish and combative with
galaxies conquering other galaxies,
meteors and comets destroying planets,
the eternal wars of the universe.

From: Pegasus, 2015. Summer/Autumn issue,
Kentucky State Poetry Society: 23

$\mathcal{D}$o We Really Have Contact?

We worship a force outside ourselves
pleading for its help to grant our wishes.
Rituals to please the great ones
often in the form of idols in stone.

The ancient ones thought the sun
brought production and harvest of food,
but also gave them floods, fire and plagues
to destroy what had already been given.

Is this power in the mysterious dark matter,
yet to be determined,
that controls the energy of the universe
oblivious to prayers asking for forgiveness?

Is the universe, so complex and extreme,
once started never to stop or be reversed?
It there purpose to praying
when no answers will come?

My You're Different

My you're different from the rest,
you don't even know how to dress.
Your name is all right, but gosh you think
we don't like you; we think you stink.

Love between two people is thought to be
all right, if they have heterogeneity,
but if your friendship seems to go
beyond the norm: "Gosh, he's homo!"

Look! I wear a label, can't you see?
I'm a believer in Christianity.
You do not look at what I do,
nor shall you list to words I spew,
but read only the believer's badge.

"You have a following, " it is said
that will give you honor and glory instead,
but what good is that little pin
when that which counts lies within?

$\mathcal{N}$ever Trust A Friend

Never trust a friend
whoever he may be.
Friends are so unpredictable
as a woman's loyalty.

But an enemy holds true.
You know what to expect:
remarks, course and snide, the blade.
Deception is never met.

Never expect to receive
an unselfish love, their best.
Then never a broken heart
will you find within your breast.

The foe must be forever watched,
so neither knife or arms,
which you know he does conceal,
has a chance to do you harm.

Smiles and words are so deceiving,
many a friendship are won with them,
but behind these false expressions
lies a selfish, dark deception.

A man who says he hates you
is a true friend indeed.
So lay you there your trust
and plant a friendship seed.

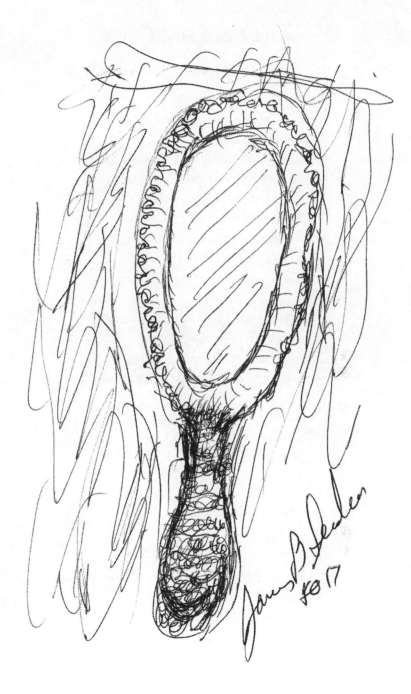

The Looking Glass

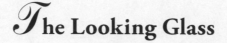The Looking Glass

As I gaze through the looking glass
to the other side of the reflective pane,
there is a world of peace and quiet there,
where dreams come true and rest is assured.

This is where hope and love reside,
this is where we can escape and hide
from the challenges of every day,
and the ever present pain of reality.

There is no other side of the mirror.
I only see my reflection there.
It is only within our imagination
we find freedom from our anxious lives.

Time

Seven months are like seven hours,
seven hours are like seven months,
and the universe heralds not the new year.
A new century is celebrated by humans alone.

The metronome swings away the minutes.
My watch's hand jumps like a trapped animal.
The sun scurries across the cloud-ridden sky
and the seasons cannot wait their turn.

How short our breath and yet it is one lifetime.
How quick the heart beats and yet so limited.
The child pushes and pulls at his robes,
but the pace of space is not changed.

We are fatigued and would like to rest.
We must pause from what we rush to complete.
There is no time, we are told, we exist
only in a space/time continuum.

"From where did you come? " asked the youth.
The father answered: "I came from nowhere.
We are all from nowhere but here, and we go nowhere.
You're the universe's child, but we are your father and mother."

Where Does Evil Dwell?

The universe knows no evil
nor does it give rise to wickedness.
Nature knows no evil fate or spirits
to lead us in unsavory ways.

We declare evil is a supernatural force
giving rise to demons, the devil,
witches and warlocks and those
who try to lead us into wicked ways.

Shamans and priests, social workers
and ministers, holy men and prophets
tell us how to fight and win
the war against the evil ones.

The battle between them and us
is not fought in open combat
but within us where evil dwells
waiting to penetrate our defenses.

Who Is A Creator?

The job of creating is one for everyone
not only by the hand and mind of God.

Each can develop something new
to be used or shared with others,
friends, family and the needy.

The gift may be as large as a life or
a kind thought given to help another.

Each can create an idea ne'er known before,
an insight into a problem thus solved
assisting self or others with insights anew.

Like the discover of the formula, E=mc2,
giving mankind hope for the future.

From: My Name is James. 2017. AuthorHouse, Bloomington, IN.

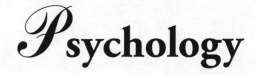
Psychology

All Are Outsiders

A waif peers through a toy store window.
A homeless one watches others dine.
A prisoner looks at those who are free.
An adict views life through distorted lenses.

These are the eccentric, the exceptional,
those living and thinking outside the norm,
different from others not of their ilk,
never becoming one of the crowd.

Their genes dictate their idiosyncracies,
never accepted into the whole of society,
ostracized in many ways from their peers.
knowing they cannot change.

Outsiders have little choice but to cling
to kindred souls for solace,
ignoring the populace, being a loner,
living at the edge of the bowl of conformity.

From: My Name is James. 2017. AuthorHouse, Bloomington, IN.

Alone And Afraid

Alone And Afraid

In the early morning hours,
neither fully asleep nor awake,
still dreaming.

I am walking on the streets and sidewalks
in a great city of tall buildings
with no windows or doors.

In this surrealistic scene
with colored boxes of different hues,
sizes and shapes; heights and widths
I am seeking directions to somewhere.

As I search for someone to help
I realize I am alone and afraid.

The Gay Gene

When *Homo sapiens* wore no clothes
and scavenged for their food,
they wandered about in family groups,
slept in trees or forest floor.

They never grew old, dying before 20.
Neither weddings or anniversaries were observed.
The dead and dying were left alone
to turn to dust, the soil to enrich.

The girls were mothers in their early teens,
unsure of who the sire might be,
and gave birth among the tall grasses
protected by the caring family.

Was the gay gene present in these times,
unexpressed by those who had it?
Or did they find, without mores and social laws,
same sex partners with whom to travel?

The Homeless One

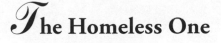

A lone daisy in a meadow broad,
or some duck lost and alone on a dusty road.
These I understand, for my heart is like them,
lonesome, alone, isolated and condemned.

If the wings of death around me wrapped,
and there were no mourner to give a rap,
then passed as "unidentified" to the table
of a medical student's studies to enable.

The young scholar no doubt would find
all the parts to hold and define,
but none could show or tell
of rich experiences now dispelled.

From: Where The Mind Dwells. Meditation.2015.
Eber and Wein, New Freedom, PA

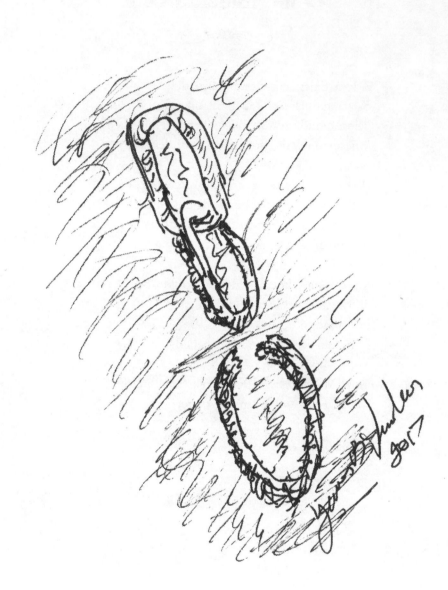

Three Links

Three Links

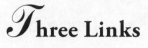

Three links were bound as one,
a solid union there.
One link was not so strong,
but did its best to share.

A stronger force than one could hold
pulled the third away.
One link, the weakest did break
from rusting and decay.

Now two links remained as one,
although they missed the third,
now the second has its wound to show
it, too, has erred and now must go.

Two Personalities

Come listen to a tale I tell
of a man born in two parts
as a bivalve in equal halves
joined together to appear as one.

Each influences the other
so different from one another
seemingly not divided
yet a fine line defines each one.

One wants to conform
to the expectations of social structure,
to belong and be approved,
loved by a woman and their offspring
accepted as part of the whole.

The other rejects customs and norms,
wants to be independent,
following his instincts and emotions
to interpret the world in his own way.

From: Pegasus. 2016. Winter/Spring issue. Kentucky
State Poetry Society. Crestview Hills, KY, 29.

Two Poems On Depression

1

I stand
on the hot desert of life.
There is no shade
from the blazing sun
of criticism.

The wind
screams:
"Thou shalt not..."
"It is unlawful to..."

Oh night!
Bring your cloak of sleep
that I might forget.

The moon
sees and knows - yes, knows -
someone knows.

2

Great mists of the unknown,
come! take this wretched mess
to the dark kingdom below.

To die.
Death - I grasp at death
as a lover,
impatient and dreaming.

From: My Name is James. 2017. AuthorHouse, Bloomington, IN.

What Is A Human?

A complex, biological robot of skin and bone
governed by spongy grey matter that knows no pain,
designed at random by natural forces
taking billions of years to complete.

A casual process begun in primordial soup
of inorganic carbon, hydrogen, oxygen, and nitrogen
stirred under high pressure and temperature
among thermal vents on the ocean floor.

This witch's brew eventually connected each
into stable, complex forms of organic compounds -
amino acids, then simple proteins -
a random, hit-or-miss, unguided process.

The process developed more complex forms
able to redesign and clone themselves.
What is a human? An unfathomable complex of chemical
interactions stimulated by electrical charges.

Sistina

Bit Of Cheese

Key words: house, mouse, cheese, cat, trap, kitchen

How quiet it is at night in the kitchen.
How quiet it is at night in the house.
This quiet is being surveyed by the cat,
who smells the fragrance of cheese
that was used to bait a trap
for the wily, cautious mouse.

Stealthy through the darkened house
with claws concealed goes the cat
through the hallway and into the kitchen
where he senses the odor of cheese,
so carefully placed securely in the trap,
as does the slowly moving mouse

All at once another smell alerts the cat.
Could it be there is a mouse
that has invaded the quiet house?
The mouse was hiding in the kitchen,
who like the cat has found the cheese.
Both determined that the cheese was in the trap.

Then the smell of the trap and cheese
from behind the cupboard in the kitchen
became mixed with another from the house.
It was that of the fat family cat
on the prowl to find the nervous mouse
before the little rodent was caught in the trap.

The prey and the stalker were to meet at the trap
in the quiet, dark behind the cupboard in the kitchen
in the middle of the night in the quiet house
over a lump of delicious cheese
that was a tasty morsel for the mouse
and the mouse a hardy meal for the cat.

$\mathcal{I}$NDEX

Printed in the United States
By Bookmasters